MAY

	Frank	Molly	Ben	
23 Monday	8.30 Give Blood — Working Late	TOOTHBRUSHES — Buy seeds — DENTIST 4:30 →	Take Sims to Jemal	HUGE MATHS TEST!! → — Birthday Presents for Grandad
24 Tuesday		GOVS meeting 8pm	Tennis	Remember ~~Jacqueline, Lawson~~ — Becky after school — mum JAFFACAKES cuttlefish
25 Wednesday	Phoe Stan Badminton 7.00	Finch book — Annual Review 3PM	BANDPRACTICE Scout Subs	DRAMA CLUB
26 Thursday	FINAL HOLIDAY DEPOSIT — Suit – Dry cleaners — Book Club Chloe's 8pm	{ JABS } earplugs! — Detention	Violin lesson 9:15am	
27 Friday	GUTTERS!! — Dinner with Boss EL GRECO	Lottie 8:30 (Key) — Leaflets 7.30	English Essay no chance! — Nick Ben's Walkman — Sleepover at Sarah's	BIN BAGS!!! — Dishwasher Salt
28 Saturday	7.30 Jog with Debbie — UNITED 2.30 — Make Cake	Aromatherapy TheLab 3.00	Call Megs School MAC — Odeon 6.45	Pocket money (don't forget mum!!) — Ha Ha Ben's got a girlfriend! — Wash P.E Kits
29 Sunday	DAD's 75th Royal Oak 12.15	Swimming ————		POND — → Cake!

THIS YEAR 2005

JANUARY
M 3 10 17 24 31
T 4 11 18 25
W 5 12 19 26
T 6 13 20 27
F 7 14 21 28
S 1 8 15 22 29
S 2 9 16 23 30

FEBRUARY
M 7 14 21 28
T 1 8 15 22
W 2 9 16 23
T 3 10 17 24
F 4 11 18 25
S 5 12 19 26
S 6 13 20 27

MARCH
M 7 14 21 28
T 1 8 15 22 29
W 2 9 16 23 30
T 3 10 17 24 31
F 4 11 18 25
S 5 12 19 26
S 6 13 20 27

JULY
M 4 11 18 25
T 5 12 19 26
W 6 13 20 27
T 7 14 21 28
F 1 8 15 22 29
S 2 9 16 23 30
S 3 10 17 24 31

AUGUST
M 1 8 15 22 29
T 2 9 16 23 30
W 3 10 17 24 31
T 4 11 18 25
F 5 12 19 26
S 6 13 20 27
S 7 14 21 28

SEPTEMBER
M 5 12 19 26
T 6 13 20 27
W 7 14 21 28
T 1 8 15 22 29
F 2 9 16 23 30
S 3 10 17 24
S 4 11 18 25

APRIL
M 4 11 18 25
T 5 12 19 26
W 6 13 20 27
T 7 14 21 28
F 1 8 15 22 29
S 2 9 16 23 30
S 3 10 17 24

MAY
M 2 9 16 23 30
T 3 10 17 24 31
W 4 11 18 25
T 5 12 19 26
F 6 13 20 27
S 7 14 21 28
S 1 8 15 22 29

JUNE
M 6 13 20 27
T 7 14 21 28
W 1 8 15 22 29
T 2 9 16 23 30
F 3 10 17 24
S 4 11 18 25
S 5 12 19 26

OCTOBER
M 3 10 17 24 31
T 4 11 18 25
W 5 12 19 26
T 6 13 20 27
F 7 14 21 28
S 1 8 15 22 29
S 2 9 16 23 30

NOVEMBER
M 7 14 21 28
T 1 8 15 22 29
W 2 9 16 23 30
T 3 10 17 24
F 4 11 18 25
S 5 12 19 26
S 6 13 20 27

DECEMBER
M 5 12 19 26
T 6 13 20 27
W 7 14 21 28
T 1 8 15 22 29
F 2 9 16 23 30
S 3 10 17 24 31
S 4 11 18 25

The phases of the moon will be indicated thus:-
● NEW MOON ☽ FIRST QUARTER ○ FULL MOON ☾ LAST QUARTER

NEXT YEAR 2006

JANUARY
M 2 9 16 23 30
T 3 10 17 24 31
W 4 11 18 25
T 5 12 19 26
F 6 13 20 27
S 7 14 21 28
S 1 8 15 22 29

FEBRUARY
M 6 13 20 27
T 7 14 21 28
W 1 8 15 22
T 2 9 16 23
F 3 10 17 24
S 4 11 18 25
S 5 12 19 26

MARCH
M 6 13 20 27
T 7 14 21 28
W 1 8 15 22 29
T 2 9 16 23 30
F 3 10 17 24 31
S 4 11 18 25
S 5 12 19 26

APRIL
M 3 10 17 24
T 4 11 18 25
W 5 12 19 26
T 6 13 20 27
F 7 14 21 28
S 1 8 15 22 29
S 2 9 16 23 30

MAY
M 1 8 15 22 29
T 2 9 16 23 30
W 3 10 17 24 31
T 4 11 18 25
F 5 12 19 26
S 6 13 20 27
S 7 14 21 28

JUNE
M 5 12 19 26
T 6 13 20 27
W 7 14 21 28
T 1 8 15 22 29
F 2 9 16 23 30
S 3 10 17 24
S 4 11 18 25

JULY
M 3 10 17 24 31
T 4 11 18 25
W 5 12 19 26
T 6 13 20 27
F 7 14 21 28
S 1 8 15 22 29
S 2 9 16 23 30

AUGUST
M 7 14 21 28
T 1 8 15 22 29
W 2 9 16 23 30
T 3 10 17 24 31
F 4 11 18 25
S 5 12 19 26
S 6 13 20 27

SEPTEMBER
M 4 11 18 25
T 5 12 19 26
W 6 13 20 27
T 7 14 21 28
F 1 8 15 22 29
S 2 9 16 23 30
S 3 10 17 24

OCTOBER
M 2 9 16 23 30
T 3 10 17 24 31
W 4 11 18 25
T 5 12 19 26
F 6 13 20 27
S 7 14 21 28
S 1 8 15 22 29

NOVEMBER
M 6 13 20 27
T 7 14 21 28
W 1 8 15 22 29
T 2 9 16 23 30
F 3 10 17 24
S 4 11 18 25
S 5 12 19 26

DECEMBER
M 4 11 18 25
T 5 12 19 26
W 6 13 20 27
T 7 14 21 28
F 1 8 15 22 29
S 2 9 16 23 30
S 3 10 17 24 31

Published by The Dodo Pad Ltd. PO Box 34330 London NW6 2RJ
Compilation & Original Illustration by Naomi McBride 2004
Illustrations © Dodo Pad Ltd 2004 © B M Peak 1995, 2004 © Rose Verney 1965, 2004

ISBN 1 903001 22 6

Amazing reprographic production by C&R Graphics, Glasgow, Scotland
Imprinted in China by Man Sang

1966   2005

Ladies AND Gentlemen!
Once again, FOR your
Delectation AND Dodelight, NOT
to Mention the EASE and
Efficiency he Brings to your Daily
Life, Lord Dodo of Doodle is
Paralactically Pleased to Present

THE

2005 Dodo-Pad

With yet another Delirious
Dodistillation of Mellifluous Musings,
Querulous Quotes, Demoded Dodefinitions
and Delusional Dodoodles

This Dodo Pad
is irreplaceable ~
if found, please return to

DOODLING

Special facilities have been made in the design of the
DODO-PAD for this essential activity. The DODO-PAD
encourages you to doodle <u>creatively</u> and thereby preserve the
covers of telephone directories, the butcher's bill, other
people's books, etc. Those normally inhibited from doodling
while they telephone will find suggestive hints to quicken
their imagination on every diary page. A blank, or nearly
blank, space is also provided for this purpose on facing
pages.

FURTHER USES FOR THE DODO-PAD

Finished sheets can be torn out and are specially suitable
for making paper boats, darts, book-markers or spills for
lighting a pipe. If folded into eight, a DODO-PAD page
comes in handy for wedging up a rickety table or stuffing
into a shaky sash-window.
    The most attractively doodled pages make a personal type
of Christmas card.

INSECTICIDE

The DODO-PAD makes an ideal weapon for swatting flies.
Held flat on the palm of the hand, it can also be
used as a missile against wasps and mosquitoes on the
ceiling.

The DODO-PAD is so designed that it may be carried in a
shopping basket or kept chained to the telephone (for
instructions how to chain your DODO-PAD to the telephone
see para. on opposite page).

A BURGLAR DISTRACTOR

''While he was giggling over my DODO-PAD I was able to
get dressed and call the police'' (name supplied).

DODO-PAD ALBUMS

If, at the end of a year, you wish to keep what amounts to a
unique record of your, or your family's, conscious and
unconscious experience, we supply leather-bound folders with
gold embossed lettering. Prices from £169.50.

CHRISTMAS AND BIRTHDAYS

Extra pages are provided at the end to facilitate the
systematic giving, or receipt, of presents. And for playing ...

THE DODO-PAD GAME

Time can be pleasantly spent, while waiting for long-
distance calls, by imagining yourself as some well-known
personality and filling in his or her engagements. But bear
in mind the laws of libel, if your DODO-PAD is liable to
be seen by others outside the family circle.

HOW TO CHAIN YOUR DODO-PAD TO THE TELEPHONE

Any reputable ironmonger will supply you with a length of
thin chain. A DODO-PADLOCK can be obtained from us.
Price £129.99, including postage.

DODO-PADLERS ARE ADVISED TO ORDER
THEIR NEXT YEAR'S DODO-PAD WELL IN
ADVANCE TO BE SURE OF SAFE DELIVERY

2005

JANUARY 2005

1 S	NEW YEAR'S DAY	17 M	MARTIN LUTHER KING DAY (U.S.)
2 Su	PUBLIC HOLIDAY, NZ	18 T	
3 M		19 W	
4 T		20 Th	
5 W		21 F	
6 Th		22 S	
7 F		23 Su	
8 S		24 M	
9 Su		25 T	
10 M		26 W	AUSTRALIA DAY
11 T		27 Th	
12 W		28 F	
13 Th		29 S	
14 F		30 Su	
15 S		31 M	
16 Su			

FEBRUARY 2005

1 T		17 Th	
2 W		18 F	
3 Th		19 S	
4 F		20 Su	
5 S		21 M	PRESIDENT'S DAY (U.S)
6 Su	WAITANGI DAY, NZ	22 T	
7 M		23 W	
8 T		24 Th	
9 W		25 F	
10 Th		26 S	
11 F		27 Su	
12 S		28 M	
13 Su			
14 M			
15 T			
16 W			

Public Holidays et al.
This information is correct at time
of going to press. The publishers
accept no responsibility for any errors.

MARCH 2005

1 T		17 Th	
2 W		18 F	
3 Th		19 S	
4 F		20 Su	
5 S		21 M	
6 Su		22 T	
7 M		23 W	
8 T		24 Th	
9 W		25 F	GOOD FRIDAY
10 Th		26 S	
11 F		27 Su	EASTER SUNDAY
12 S		28 M	EASTER MONDAY
13 Su		29 T	
14 M	COMMONWEALTH DAY, AUS	30 W	
15 T		31 Th	
16 W			

APRIL 2005

1 F		17 Su	
2 S		18 M	
3 Su		19 T	
4 M		20 W	
5 T		21 Th	
6 W		22 F	
7 Th		23 S	
8 F		24 Su	
9 S		25 M	ANZAC DAY
10 Su		26 T	
11 M		27 W	
12 T		28 Th	
13 W		29 F	
14 Th		30 S	
15 F			
16 S			

MAY 2005

1 Su		17 T	
2 M	MAY HOLIDAY, UK + REP. IRELAND	18 W	
3 T		19 Th	
4 W		20 F	
5 Th		21 S	
6 F		22 Su	
7 S		23 M	
8 Su		24 T	
9 M		25 W	
10 T		26 Th	
11 W		27 F	
12 Th		28 S	
13 F		29 Su	
14 S		30 M	MEMORIAL DAY (U.S.) BANK HOLIDAY, UK
15 Su		31 T	
16 M			

JUNE 2005

1 W		17 F	
2 Th		18 S	
3 F		19 Su	
4 S		20 M	
5 Su		21 T	
6 M	QUEEN'S BIRTHDAY, NZ	22 W	
7 T		23 Th	
8 W		24 F	
9 Th		25 S	
10 F		26 Su	
11 S		27 M	LABOUR DAY, NZ
12 Su		28 T	
13 M		29 W	
14 T		30 Th	
15 W			
16 Th			

2005

JULY 2005		
1 F	17 Su	
2 S	18 M	
3 Su	19 T	
4 M	INDEPENDENCE DAY, USA	20 W	
5 T	21 Th	
6 W	22 F	
7 Th	23 S	
8 F	24 Su	
9 S	25 M	
10 Su	26 T	
11 M	27 W	
12 T	28 Th	
13 W	29 F	
14 Th	30 S	
15 F	31 Su	
16 S		

AUGUST 2005		
1 M	17 W	
2 T	18 Th	
3 W	19 F	
4 Th	20 S	
5 F	21 Su	
6 S	22 M	
7 Su	23 T	
8 M	24 W	
9 T	25 Th	
10 W	26 F	
11 Th	27 S	
12 F	28 Su	
13 S	29 M	BANK HOLIDAY, UK
14 Su	30 T	
15 M	31 W	
16 T		

SEPTEMBER 2005		
1 Th	17 S	
2 F	18 Su	
3 S	19 M	
4 Su	20 T	
5 M	LABOR DAY, USA	21 W	
6 T	22 Th	
7 W	23 F	
8 Th	24 S	
9 F	25 Su	
10 S	26 M	
11 Su	27 T	
12 M	28 W	
13 T	29 Th	
14 W	30 F	
15 Th		
16 F		

OCTOBER 2005		
1 S	17 M	
2 Su	18 T	
3 M	19 W	
4 T	20 Th	
5 W	21 F	
6 Th	22 S	
7 F	23 Su	
8 S	24 M	
9 Su	25 T	
10 M	COLUMBUS DAY (U.S.)	26 W	
11 T	27 Th	
12 W	28 F	
13 Th	29 S	
14 F	30 Su	
15 S	31 M	
16 Su		

NOVEMBER 2005		
1 Tu	17 Th	
2 W	18 F	
3 Th	19 S	
4 F	20 Su	
5 S	21 M	
6 Su	22 T	
7 M	23 W	
8 T	24 Th	
9 W	25 F	THANKSGIVING, USA
10 Th	26 S	
11 F	VETERANS' DAY (U.S)	27 Su	
12 S	28 M	
13 Su	29 T	
14 M	30 W	
15 T		
16 W		

DECEMBER 2005		
1 Th	17 S	
2 F	18 Su	
3 S	19 M	
4 Su	20 T	
5 M	21 W	
6 T	22 Th	
7 W	23 F	
8 Th	24 S	
9 F	25 Su	CHRISTMAS DAY
10 S	26 M	BOXING DAY
11 Su	27 T	
12 M	28 W	
13 T	29 Th	
14 W	30 F	
15 Th	31 S	
16 F		

"Most modern calendars mar
the sweet simplicity of our
lives by reminding us that
each day that passes is the
anniversary of some perfectly
uninteresting event"
                    Oscar Wilde

But not, of course, the Dodo
Pad, which strives annually
to do exactly the opposite.
                    Lord Dodo of Doodle

2004 // 2005

DEC // JAN

27 Monday

28 Tuesday

29 Wednesday

30 Thursday

31 Friday

1 Saturday — New Year's Day

2 Sunday

NO PICKNICKING

TOURISTS CAN OBTAIN
A BETTER VIEW FROM
THE TOP OF THE
OPPOSITE PAGE
BY ORDER OF
TELANISSUS R.D.C.

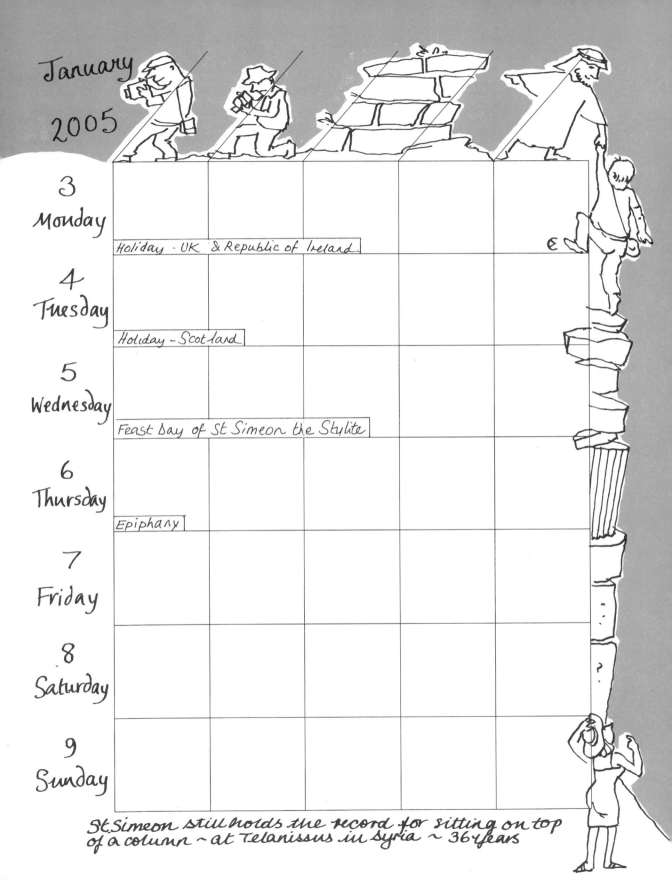

January

2005

3 Monday

Holiday - UK & Republic of Ireland

4 Tuesday

Holiday - Scotland

5 Wednesday

Feast Day of St Simeon the Stylite

6 Thursday

Epiphany

7 Friday

8 Saturday

9 Sunday

St. Simeon still holds the record for sitting on top
of a column ~ at Telanissus in Syria ~ 36 years

Dodelusional Notions of Immortality

T.H. White, author of The Sword and the Stone (and much else) was a tall impressive man with a white beard. Once, answering the door-bell of his house in Alderney he was confronted by a group of Jehovah's Witnesses asking for money.
"Splendid," he said. "I AM Jehovah! How are we doing?"

General de Gaulle was asked if he would like a state funeral when he died. "No," he said, "it would be a waste of money; I shall only be gone for three days."

January
2005

10
Monday

11
Tuesday

12
Wednesday

13
Thursday

14
Friday

15
Saturday

16
Sunday

ISA'S BED

I love in Isa's bed to lie,
Oh such a joy and luxury!
The bottom of the bed I sleep,
And with great care within I creep;
Oft I embrace her feet of lillys,
but she has goton all the pillys.
Her neck I never can embrace,
But I do hug her feet in place..

'Pet'Marjorie Fleming,
child poet
from Kirkaldy, Fife,
who died aged 8 years.

Marjorie was a distant relative through
marriage of Sir Walter Scott, whom she
captivated with her ingenuous bright wit.
He apparently called her his "wee bonnie
croodlin' do", and said
"She's the most extraordinary creature I ever
met with, and her repeating of Shakespeare
overpowers me as nothing else does".

January

2005

17
Monday

Martin Luther King Day (US)

18
Tuesday

19
Wednesday

1811 Death of 'Pet' Marjorie Fleming

20
Thursday

21
Friday

22
Saturday

23
Sunday

DODORNITHOLOGY CORNER

"Bred any good rooks lately?"

A scientist recently crossed a carrier pigeon
with a woodpecker.
He bred a bird that not only delivers messages
to their dodestination, but knocks on the
door when he gets there.

January
2005

24
Monday

25
Tuesday — BURNS NIGHT ⭕

26
Wednesday — AUSTRALIA DAY

27
Thursday

28
Friday

29
Saturday

30
Sunday

The early bird catches the worm, but the second mouse gets the cheese

*Advice to those who try
to supplement their diet
from Nature's larder :—*

DON'T cook and attempt to eat young
bracken shoots because the Japanese do.
What suits the hardy races of the extreme
East may not suit you.

NB:- Mice in honey should be imported
from China, not prepared at home.

The Weekend Book 1931

FEBRUARY 2005

31 January
Monday

1 Tuesday

2 Wednesday

3 Thursday

4 Friday

5 Saturday

6 Sunday

1865 Isabella Mary Beeton died | WAITANGI DAY, N.Z.

Fortune Cookie for Chinese New Year

You are only young once. After that,
you have to think up some other
excuse.

FORTUNE COOKIE DE NOS JOURS
The moving cursor writes, and having writ, blinks on ....

February 2005

7 Monday

8 Tuesday
Shrove Tuesday

9 Wednesday
Ash Wednesday | Chinese New Year

10 Thursday
Muslim New Year

11 Friday

12 Saturday

13 Sunday

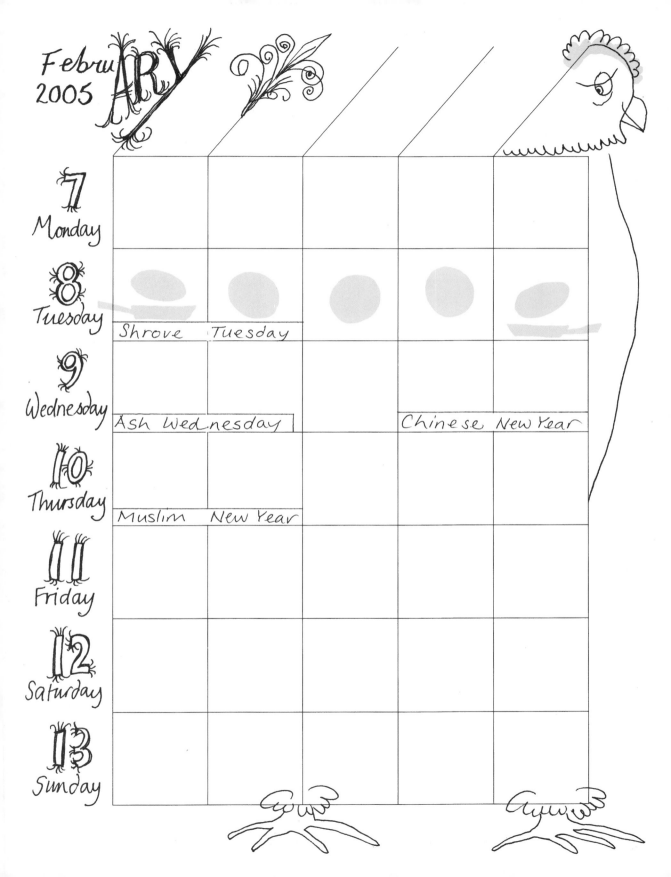

On Valentine's Day
Will a good goose lay
~ English Proverb

February 2005

14
Monday

15
Tuesday

16
Wednesday

17
Thursday

18
Friday

19
Saturday

20
Sunday

No two snowflakes are ever the same.
For some structured doodling, why
not create a few of your own. Here
are some shapes to start you off —

Out Now - cutting edge technology for a new life in the slow lane

Here at Dodo Towers, a team of Sharp Cards and Proverbial Mugs has been hard at work, preparing for the launch of the latest and most brilliant of all Lord Dodo's inventions – The Nonlinear Opt-in Text Editor for Bio-Optically Organized Knowledge, or NOTEBOOK for short. This revolutionary new storage device – the Dodo Blank Book - has no wires, no chips, no motherboards (or bored mothers), no crashes, no boots, no freezes. Sheets of wood pulp are bound and ordered sequentially. Each sheet is capable of storing thousands of bytes of information. The Dodo Blank Book works in all weathers and terrain from desert to tundra, temperate to arctic and is impervious to viruses, worms, magnetic fields and idiot operators. Could Michaelangelo have gone into ceiling design without one? Would Lord Dodo have remembered to pay the plumber to fix the Cistern in his Chapel? Did Einstein need a laptop for his Grand Unified Theory of Relatives? Where does your mother store her shopping list? Whether you're a budding Goya or Graffiti veteran, whether your calling is Grub Street or a Dusty Garret, whether your Grand Oeuvre is a Penny Dreadful or a Dollar Earner, or your Concerto for One Band Napping a hit or a miss, the Dodo Blank Book will always be at hand to save your ruminations and musings from oblivion. *Size: 6" x 8½" 160 pages*

Dodon't-Forget...

NEW - Dodo Sticky Notes - Do Do Remember: Dodon't-Forget-me-Notes. 4 sticky notepads of 50 pages each with a FREE postcard.

NEW - The Dodo Door Pad - Out of sorts, but not out of doors? Then get a handle on your affairs and hang out your troubles and wares, lists and memos for all to see. It's time to let Lord Dodo show you the door with this hang-it-out-to-dodo memory jogger. *Size: 9" x 3¾" 75 sheets*

ALL TIME FAVOURITES FROM AN OLD MASTER

Lord Dodo's other Dodorganisers – whether you're at the stove, on the road or down on your knees in the garden, you can stay on the ball with the Book for Cooks, the Travel Log and the Book of Garden Cuttings. Each is equipped with pockets, pouches and dividers to help you stuff and store those recipes, mementos and cuttings that would otherwise disappear forever. No more past imperfect and tense present. Get a future perfect and get a grip by investing in the Dodo Pad's brilliant dodon't be forgetful range of diaries, organizers and memory joggers.

(See pages following w/c 12th September for more about your "can't-live-without-em" dodo favourites)

Sharp Cards and Proverbial Mugs

Lord Dodo has collected 12 proverbs from around the globe and herewith presents them for your delectation: As mugs – for everyday drinking and refreshment. As cards – for every occasion and anniversary.

(Please see pages following w/c 12th September for full details)

*10% off all orders over £25 received between 1 January – 31 March 2005. To receive your 10% discount, please quote 'Spring in the Air offer 04RD' when you order. See order form overleaf for contact information and how to order.

Name (please PRINT)

Address

Postcode /Zip   Tel No (in case of query)   Day/Eve

E-mail

Dodon't Forget Range & Dodorganisers		No. required	£ Total
DBB	NEW! Dodo Blank Book @ £8.95		
SNP	NEW! Dodo Sticky Notes (4 pads) @ £7.50		
DHP	NEW! Dodo Door Pad @ £5.50		
MMB	Wipe-clean Memo Board @ £4.50		
DTL	Dodo Travel Log @ £16.50		
DGB	Dodo Book of Garden Cuttings @ £17.95		
DBC	Dodo Book for Cooks @ £17.95		
ADB	Maxi Dodo Address Book @ £12.95 NEW DURABLE COVER!		
ADBM	Mini Dodo Address Book @ £8.50 NEW DURABLE COVER!		

Dodo Proverbial Mugs in Bone China @ £7.75			No. required	£ Total
DMS	Mug – Spanish	*How beautiful it is to do…*		
DMF	Mug – French	*It's always the impossible…*		
DMA	Mug – African	*Cross the river before you…*		
DMC	Mug – Chinese	*The birds of sadness…*		
DMU	Mug – American	*Some days you're the…*		
DMJ	Mug – Japanese	*Daylight will peep through…*		
DMB	Mug – Barbadian	*The new broom sweeps…*		
DMI	Mug – Irish	*Take the drink for the…*		
DMY	Mug – Yiddish	*One chops the wood…*		
DMM	Mug – Madagascan	*Don't think of the shortness…*		
DMG	Mug – Chinese	*All gardeners know better…*		
DML	Mug – Old Lore	*Pray to God but keep rowing…*		

Greetings Cards – order in multiples of 3 – mix & match at your whim!

☐ A – Spanish   ☐ B – French   ☐ C – African   ☐ D – Chinese

☐ E – American   ☐ F – Japanese   ☐ G – Barbadian   ☐ H – Irish

☐ J – Yiddish   ☐ K – Madagascan   ☐ L – Chinese   ☐ M – Old Lore

3 @ £4.95	
6 @ £9.90	
9 @ £14.85	
12 @ £18.00	

Please see below for Overseas Postage Supplements*

All prices shown above are <u>inclusive</u> of UK delivery. *Overseas postage supplements:
Please add £1.75 per copy/item for non-UK European mail and world-wide surface mail.
Add £2.75 per copy/item for world-wide airmail. NB: Greetings Cards do not attract
postage supplements. Bulk order prices on application.

I enclose a crossed cheque/postal order payable to *The Dodo Pad Ltd*
OR *Please debit my Visa/Mastercard/American Express/Switch account no:*

Grand Total £

(Switch only)

Start Date   Issue No.

Expiry date   USA and overseas orders: If you are paying with a non-UK credit card, your account will be
debited with the UK sterling equivalent at the time of order fulfilment.

Signature   Date

You can order from Lord Dodo in any of following ways:
Visit our web site: www.dodopad.com and order securely online
Order by e-mail: mailorder@dodopad.com
Mail Order telephone hotline: 0870 900 8004 (BT national call rates apply)
Order by post: The Dodo Pad, PO Box 34330, London, NW6 2RJ
Order by Fax: +44 (0) 870 750 3051 (BT national call rates apply)

For dodoffice use only   04RD

We aim to dispatch within 7 days of receipt of your order but please allow up to 21 days for delivery. Subject to availability.

*10% off all orders over £25 received between 1st January and 31st March 2005.

FEBRUARY 2005

21 MONDAY

22 TUESDAY

23 WEDNESDAY

24 THURSDAY

25 FRIDAY

26 SATURDAY

27 SUNDAY

President's Day (U.S.)

"The most serious charge that can be laid against New England is not Puritanism, but February." *Mark Twain*

LORD DODO'S TIP FOR
HOUSEHOLD MANAGEMENT

As carried out by the indoor
staff at Dodo Towers

Traditionally, fleas start to
appear on 1st March, so rise at
dawn, fling the windows open and
sweep the house from top to
bottom, keeping all the windows
firmly closed afterwards.

What's this ?

FEB MAR
2005

28 Monday

Tuesday

2 Wednesday

3 Thursday

4 Friday

5 Saturday

6 Sunday

St David's Day

Mothering Sunday U.K.

A worm climbing over a razor blade

Lrod Ddoo of Dodloe is
dleigthed to arawd the
uasul Ddoo Pad to
Sue Pretty for the floolwnig
osrebavoitn

'Aoccdrnig to rscheearch at an Elingsh uinervtisy, it deosn't mttaer in
waht oredr the ltteers in a wrod are, the olny iprmoetnt tihng is taht
the frist and lsat ltteer is at the rghit pclae. The rset can be a
toatlmses and you can sitll raed it wouthit porbelm. Tihs is bcuseae we
donot raed ervey lteter by it slef but the wrod as a wlohe.'

DID YOU HEAR ABOUT THE MAN WHO STOLE SOME RHUBARB?

MARCH

2005

7 Monday

8 Tuesday

9 Wednesday

10 Thursday

11 Friday

12 Saturday

13 Sunday

THE POLICE TOOK HIM INTO CUSTARDY

L'Art Deaudeau

Lady Dodo levitates during a
particularly exciting séance at
Dodo Towers(Lord Dodo is up in
town).

March 2005

14 Monday — Commonwealth Day

15 Tuesday

16 Wednesday — Death of Aubrey Beardsley 1898

17 Thursday — St Patrick's Day ~ Holiday | N. Ireland & | Republic of Ireland | ℈

18 Friday

19 Saturday

20 Sunday — Palm Sunday

In spite of their hats being very ugly, Goddam! I love the English.

Beranger, 1814

Here are some lovelies who need hats. Will you oblige...

Miss Frizell   "Lola"   Duane

MARCH 2005

21
Monday — Spring Equinox

22
Tuesday

23
Wednesday

24
Thursday

25
Friday — Good Friday   ○

26
Saturday

27
Sunday — Easter Sunday   British Summer Time begins *

*correct at time of going to press

On COGITO; ERGO SUM

There once was a man who said "God
Must find it exceedingly odd
   If he finds that this tree
   Continues to be
When there's no-one about in the quad."

Ronald Knox

A REPLY

Dear Sir,
     Your astonishment's odd
I am always about in the quad
   And that's why the tree
   Continues to be
Since observed by
       Yours faithfully,
        God.

Anon.

THE YOUNG DODESCARTES COGITATING HIS SUMS

MARCH~
APRIL
2005

28 Monday

Bank Holiday UK & Republic of Ireland

29 Tuesday

30 Wednesday

31 Thursday

1596 René Descartes born

1 Friday

2 Saturday

3 Sunday

MACKEREL IS IN SEASON WHEN BALAAM'S ASS SPEAKS IN CHURCH
Second Sunday after Lent when, in the Old Lectionary, the first
lesson was Numbers XXII

A nervous wreck.

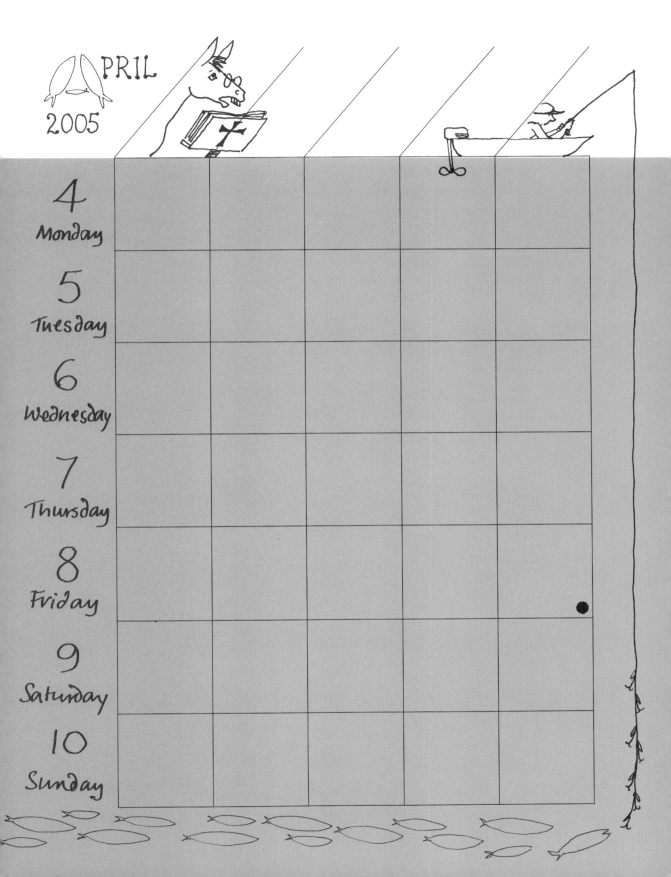

APRIL
2005

4 Monday				
5 Tuesday				
6 Wednesday				
7 Thursday				
8 Friday				
9 Saturday				
10 Sunday				

Some other interesting international monsters
as listed by Lord Dodo's old friend Heinz Mode
in "Fabulous Beasts and Dodemons":-

THE PSEZPOLNICA, a Wendish (Slavic German)
horse-footed witch who beheads any passer-by
who cannot talk for one hour about flax.

THE BURMESE WATER-ELEPHANT, as small as a
mouse but of enormous strength, which feeds
on the brains of mormal-sized elephants.

THE ICELANDIC SKOFFIN, a
cross between a tomcat and a
vixen, whose gaze is fatal.

CHERUFELS,gigantic Andean creatures that eat
girls and live in volcanoes.

Lord Dodo is fascinated to know what
these monsters look like. The usual
reward to the Dodo-padler with the
most active imagination who can
oblige.

APRIL 2005

11 Monday

12 Tuesday

13 Wednesday

14 Thursday

First modern sighting of Loch Ness Monster 1933

15 Friday

16 Saturday

17 Sunday

DODEJEUNER SUR L'HERBE

APRIL 2005

18 Monday					
19 Tuesday					
20 Wednesday	1883 Edouard Manet died				
21 Thursday					
22 Friday					
23 Saturday					
24 Sunday	Passover				○

O liberte! Que de crimes on commet en ton nom! *

It is a far, far better thing that I dodo....

* 'O Liberty! What crimes are committed in your name'
  – ascribed to Madame Roland on the scaffold

Avril
2005
& May

25 Monday

26 Tuesday

27 Wednesday

28 Thursday

29 Friday

30 Saturday

May
1 Sunday

ANZAC DAY

Dr Guillotin's improved machine is first used 1792

ENCORE DES DODEFINITIONS

Here are some dodefinitions of other familiar English
words, which are, like guillotine, derived from French
proper names. Can you identify them?

1.   Extreme patriotism or national pride.
2.   A skin-tight garment.
3.   An outline portrait.
4.   A poisonous narcotic alkaloid.
5.   A hairstyle.

Answers opposite May 23rd.

MAY
2005

2 Monday
Bank Holiday U.K. Public Holiday Rep. of Ireland

3 Tuesday

4 Wednesday

5 Thursday

6 Friday

7 Saturday
1875 First Kentucky Derby

8 Sunday
Mother's Day U.S. & Aus.

TO BEE OR NOT TO BEE

The world's largest known bee, the carpenter bee, is so
keen to find a mate that it has been known to try to seduce
anything airborne, including dandelion seeds, birds, and
even aircraft.

The government introduces sex-education classes
for carpenter bees after a rear-miss with a Boeing 747

A swarm in May
Is worth a load of hay
A swarm in June
Is worth a silver spoon
A swarm in July
Is not worth a fly

MAY

2 5

9
Monday

10
Tuesday

11
Wednesday

12
Thursday

13
Friday

14
Saturday

15
Sunday

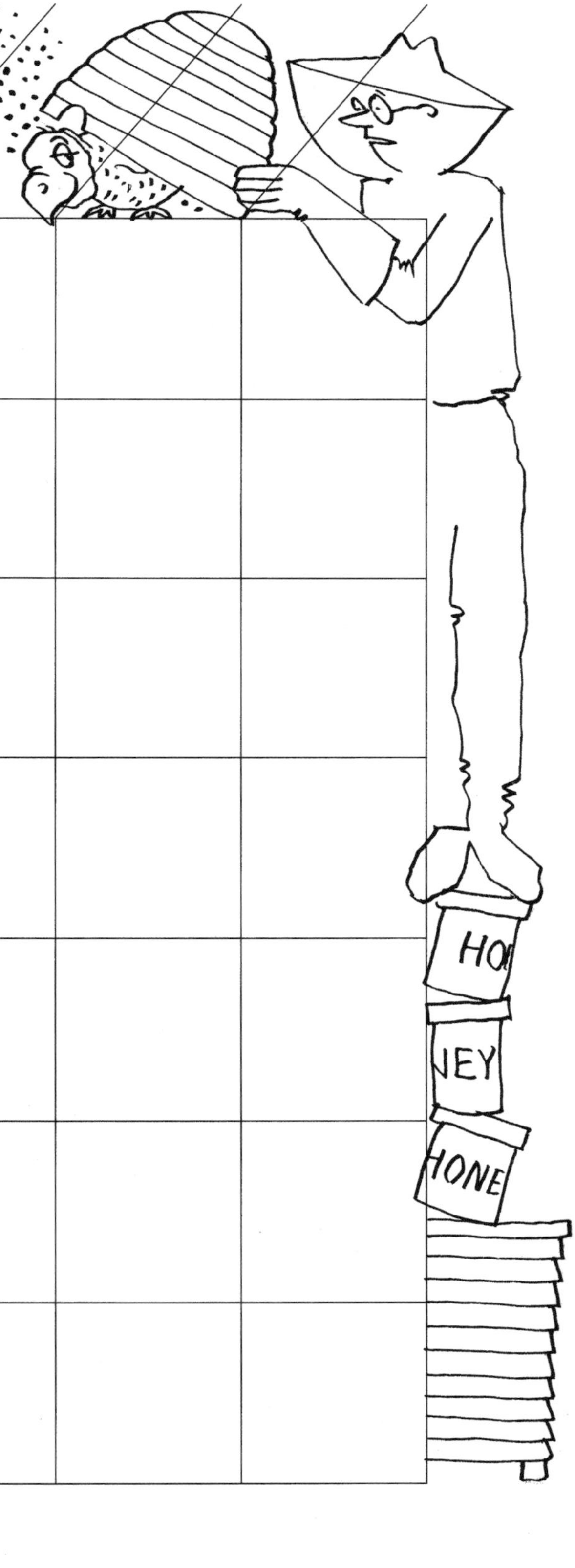

HO
JEY
HONE

MAY
2005

16 Monday

17 Tuesday

18 Wednesday

19 Thursday

Mount St. Helens erupted in Washington U.S. 1980

20 Friday

21 Saturday

22 Sunday

Can you name 2 other States in the USA that have active volcanoes?

Answers below June 12th

DODEFINITIVE ANSWERS

1 Chauvinism	From Nicolas Chauvin, a soldier who idolised Napoleon
2 Leotard	Jules Leotard (1842-70), gymnast, was the first to wear one
3 Silhouette	First drawn by Etienne de Silhouette (1709-67)
4 Nicotine	Jean Nicot (?1530-1600) first introduced tobacco to France
5 Pompadour	From Madame de Pompadour, mistress of King Louis XV

May

2005

23 Monday					O
24 Tuesday					
25 Wednesday	1803 Ralph Waldo Emerson born				
26 Thursday					
27 Friday					
28 Saturday					
29 Sunday					

IT'S OFFICIAL ~ "Nature hates calculators" ~ Ralph Waldo Emerson

How good is your botany?

SOME COMMON PLANTS

Cowslip

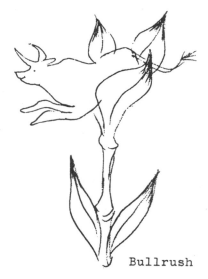

Bullrush

Buttockup

MAY & JUNE 2005

30 Monday

31 Tuesday

1 Wednesday

2 Thursday

3 Friday

4 Saturday

5 Sunday

Bank Holiday U.K.

Memorial Day U.S.

E

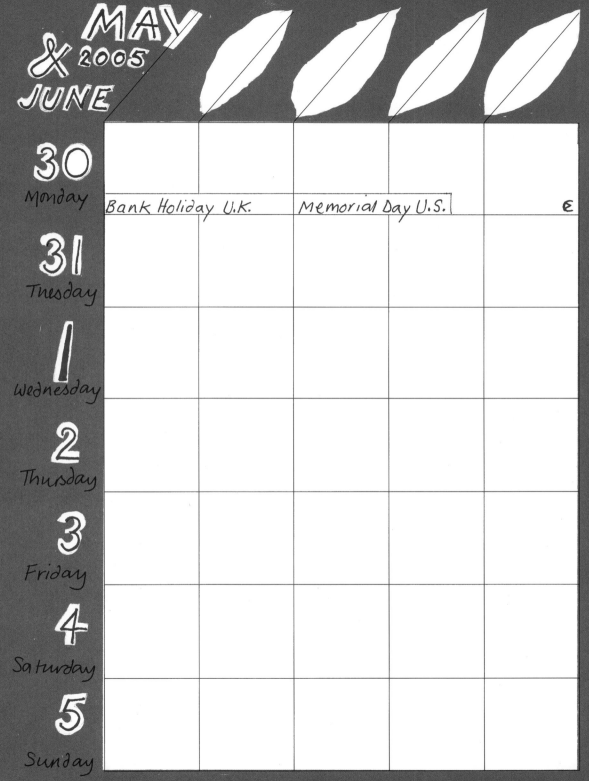

There was a young girl from Westphalia
Who went to a dance as a dahlia.
    The petals revealed
    What they should have concealed
And the dance,
        as a dance,
            was a failure.

JUNE 2005

6 Monday

7 Tuesday

8 Wednesday

9 Thursday

10 Friday

11 Saturday

12 Sunday

Holiday - Republic of Ireland	Queen's	Birthday - NZ	●

Hawaii - Mauna Loa is the world's largest active volcano.
Alaska

GREAT GROUPS

Here are some unusual names
for groups of animals, birds
and people.

Try putting the right name
to each group.

TIDINGS of	HUNTERS
SKULK of	FORESTERS
STALK of	BADGERS
CLOUD of	STARLINGS
POD of	OWLS
MORBIDITY of	MAGPIES
MURMURATION of	WHALES
PARLIAMENT of	FRIARS
BLAST of	MAJORS
COLONY of	SEAFOWL

(answers opposite August 1st)

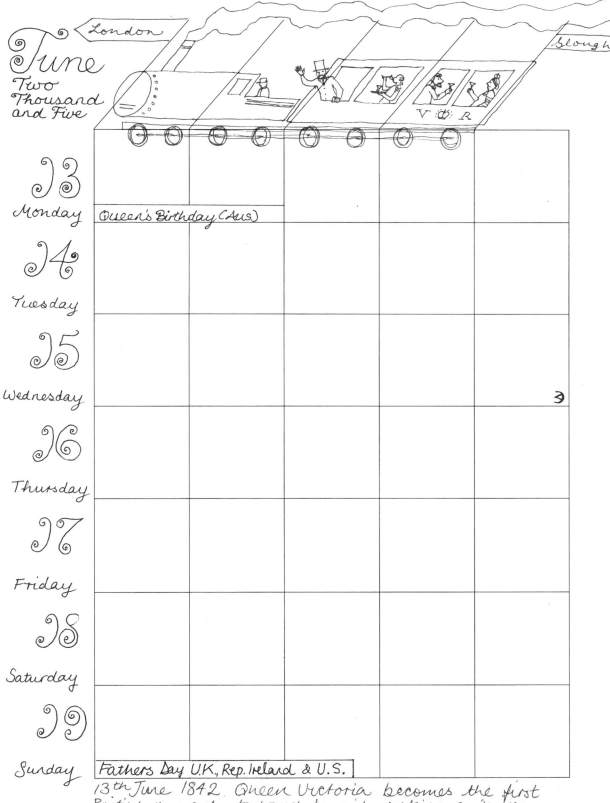

June
Two
Thousand
and Five

13
Monday
Queen's Birthday (Aus.)

14
Tuesday

15
Wednesday

16
Thursday

17
Friday

18
Saturday

19
Sunday
Fathers Day U.K., Rep. Ireland & U.S.

13th June 1842. Queen Victoria becomes the first British monarch to travel by rail, making a journey from Slough to London.

Sir Christopher Wren
Said "I am going to dine with some men.
If anyone calls
Say I am designing St Paul's".

                                    E.C.Bentley

Little known fact — Sir Christopher Wren was an early
dodevotee of the Dodo-Pad, and used it to keep minutes
of site meetings when designing St Paul's.

20 Monday

21 Tuesday

summer Solstice

22 Wednesday   O

23 Thursday

24 Friday

25 Saturday

26 Sunday

21st June 1675-work began to rebuild St Paul's
Cathedral after the Great Fire of London

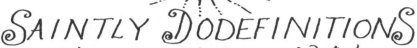

SAINTLY DODEFINITIONS

The petrel is so called because of Peter's attempt to walk on water (Matthew XIV, 29). His faith deserting him, he began to sink, and would have drowned had not Jesus come to his aid. The birds are called after Peter because they fly so low that they sometimes seem to be walking on the sea.

June/July
2005

27 Monday

28 Tuesday

29 Wednesday — Feast Day of St Peter

30 Thursday

1 Friday

2 Saturday

3 Sunday

Lord Dodo's Garden of Dodelights

"How I simply loathe watering the garden!"

2005

July

4
Monday

Independence Day U.S.

5
Tuesday

6
Wednesday

7
Thursday

8
Friday

9
Saturday

10
Sunday

Le Dodoggerel Français

When challenged to write a piece of poetry in English,
Victor Hugo penned the following:

```
Pour chasser le spleen
J'entrai dans un inn;
O, mais je bus le gin,
God save the Queen!
```

"France has neither winter nor summer nor morals. Apart from these drawbacks, it is a fine country."

Mark Twain

Ce juillet 2005

11 lundi			
12 mardi	Holiday N. Ireland		
13 mercredi			
14 jeudi	Bastille Day		ʒ
15 vendredi			
16 samedi			
17 dimanche			

LIBERTÉ·ÉGALITÉ·FRATERNITÉ

Q. What do you get when you cross a cowboy with a gourmet?

JULY 2005

18 Monday				
19 Tuesday				
20 Wednesday				
21 Thursday				O
22 Friday				
23 Saturday				
24 Sunday	1851 - window tax abolished			

A.   Hopalong casserole

Lord Dodo's page of Dodeductions

LORD DODO is so horrified by the size
of his restaurant bill that he lapses
into number talk. Can you translate
his reply into words?

3414
340
74813
_____
43374813

IF YOU DOUBT THAT THE ABOVE
ADDITION IS CORRECT – HOLD
IT UP BEFORE A MIRROR

JULY

2005

25 Monday

26 Tuesday

27 Wednesday

28 Thursday

29 Friday

30 Saturday

31 Sunday

England wins the Football World Cup 1966

GREAT GROUPS   Answers

A blast of hunters
A stalk of foresters
A colony of badgers
A murmuration of starlings
A parliament of owls
A tiding of magpies
A pod of whales
A skulk of friars
A morbidity of majors
A cloud of sea fowl

Any suggestions from Dodopaddlers for a group of Dodos?

Adventurous Rosemary Pullin-Jodson sets off on a tour of the Galapagos Islands on "Bucky"

AUGUST 2005

1 Monday	Holiday - Scotland and Republic of Ireland				
2 Tuesday					
3 Wednesday					
4 Thursday					
5 Friday					
6 Saturday					
7 Sunday					

What men call gallantry, and the Gods adultery,
Is much more common when the climate's sultry.

Lord Byron

AUGUST 2005

8 Monday

9 Tuesday

10 Wednesday

11 Thursday

12 Friday

13 Saturday

14 Sunday

There once was a gourmet of Crediton
Who ate pate-de-foie; he spread it on
A chocolate biscuit.
And said "I'll just risk it"
His tomb gives the date that he said on.   *Edward Lear*

*THE DODO PAD, on the other hand, can
be taken without the least ill effect.*

"The ones with teethmarks have hard centres."

AUGUST 2005

15 Monday

1057 Macbeth killed by Malcolm, Son of Duncan

16 Tuesday

17 Wednesday

18 Thursday

19 Friday

O

20 Saturday

21 Sunday

Lord Dodo, a man of exceptionally fine physique, saves his Dodo-Pad from dodecapods at Dodeaville.

Answer to Dodeduction from July 31st

I ought to owe nothing for I ate nothing

August
2005

22
Monday

23
Tuesday

24
Wednesday

25
Thursday

26
Friday

27
Saturday

1913 Russian Lt Peter Nesterov is first to loop the loop

28
Sunday

Chess fancy that!

Every September in the Italian town of Marostica, the inhabitants play a living game of chess in the town's checkerboard square. The tradition dates back to 1454, when this method was used to decide which of two young noblemen should have the hand of the daughter of the local notable. Not every chess piece is a person; some are police horses.

August ~ September 2005

29 Monday — Bank Holiday England Wales & N. Ireland

30 Tuesday

31 Wednesday

1 Thursday

2 Friday

3 Saturday

4 Sunday — Father's Day-Aus.

'When a man's house is burning, it is not good to play at chess'
English Proverb

Lord and Lady Dodo take a few moments off from their afternoon hack to drop in on the annual cricket match between FUDPE* and the indoor servants at Dodo Towers.

* Federated Union of Dodo Pad Employees

September 2005

5 Monday — 1826 Wisden first published   Labor Day U.S.

6 Tuesday — 1880 First Test Match at The Oval - England v. Australia

7 Wednesday

8 Thursday

9 Friday

10 Saturday

11 Sunday

3

Also on 6th August, 1776, 3 stumps were used for the first time in a match between Coulsdon and Chertsey.

Don't lose your head trying to organise your life!
Order next year's Dodo Pad today.

Or next week, anyway.
Order form coming up......

SEPTEMBER
2005

12
Monday

13
Tuesday

14
Wednesday

15
Thursday

16
Friday

17
Saturday

18
Sunday

1879 Blackpool illuminations switched on for first time

40 YEARS ON
AND STILL GOING STRONG

Dodo of Doodle, Lord High Vizier and Grand
Panjandrum of Dodo Products Ink, humbly
presents for your delectation the fortieth
anniversary edition of that monumental
memorandum and engagement journal,
that consummate compendium of
worldly wisdom, that inimitable
arbiter of household accord,
the apotheosis of diurnal
order, a paragon
without peer*
the...

Dodo-Pad

*Peer without secretary seeks general factotum to gofer and flunkey.
Would suit gullible romantic of independent means
with eye on the publishing trade.
No hand in the till merchants please.

1966 2006

The travel journal with broad horizons

THE DODO TRAVEL LOG is for wayfarers, seafarers and hitch-hikers (no-farers). Whether you're planning an expedition to Ecuador or an excursion to Eden, a perambulation in Peru or a diversion via Devizes, this nifty A5 spiral bound notebook is the way to organise your itinerary and archive your adventures. With four laminated pouched dividers, space for addresses and a clear snap-lock pouch, all your escapades

(along with your tickets, postcards and maps) can be stuffed into the pages and pockets of the Travel Log. This Voyager's Vade Mecum is the place to commit your yarns (ripping or riotous) and tales (tall or short) to paper. Lord Dodo has not only added 100 FREE photo corners and a FREE security pouch for passports,

credit cards and cash, but also a laminated wipe-clean journey jotter for daily notes as you wend your way around the world. So whether its wild moors (Yorkshire) or cultural exploration (Moorish) that set your Journeyman Genes alight, the Dodo Travel Log is the only companion for wayfarers with wanderlust and wanderers with Winnebagos. Don't be a castaway without a chronicle – make a record of your ramblings and save your wanderings from wandering. *Size: 6"x 8½" 176 pages*

Turn over a new leaf and find your green fingers

THE DODO BOOK OF GARDEN CUTTINGS will cut a swathe through those mounds of garden notes and jottings. Cultivate your own horticultural calendar and plan what-to-do-when and where-to-do-what. Divided into ten easy-to-use sections, you can file garden articles under Notes and stuff artichokes under April. Sieve those garden cuttings, jot or stick them down and sift through what you need to know month by month. With a durable wipe-clean cover to protect your horticultural inspirations from mud, mulch and manure you can organize your husbandry, from Bonfires to Begonias, with this perfect companion for gardeners with a sense of humus. Whether you're wrestling with a crabby apple or playing with tubers, THE DODO BOOK OF GARDEN CUTTINGS is the ideal Dodorganiser for Horticulturists from Eden to Ealing.
Size: 7½" x 9½" 180 pages

The Dodo Book for Cooks
THE CURE FOR LOST RECIPE SYNDROME

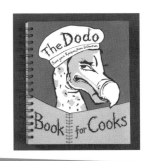

Now into its 6th reprint, this splendidly popular recipe notebook is divided into 10 sections from 'Soups and Starters' to 'Festive Fare'. Peppered throughout with amusing culinary scraps and drawings, there's plenty of space to stick and stuff those recipes. For all those frustrated by the Won't-Lie-Flat cook book, its spiral binding does not snap shut just as the soufflé subsides and the Crème brulées. A durable wipe-clean cover spares your creations from the ravages of gravy, grease and grime. *Size: 7½" x 9½" 160 pages*

'Since discovering the Dodo Book for Cooks, I have never once burnt the steak...' The Reverend T. Bone

'Get stuffed.' The Guzzler's Gazette

'Lies flat while you drink to England, France, Canada, or anywhere...' Monsieur Beaucoup Duvin

Download the lowdown at www.dodopad.com

Out Now - cutting edge technology for a new life in the slow lane

Buried in the ancient village of Much Havock-in-the-Mold, deep in the green heart of the verdant glades and valleys of Albion, lies the ancestral seat of Lord Dodo – Executive-in-Chief of Dodo Products Ink, the Global Publishing and New Media Conglomerate. Here at Dodo Towers, a team of Sharp Cards and Proverbial Mugs has been hard at work, preparing for the launch of the latest and most brilliant of all Lord Dodo's inventions – The **N**onlinear **O**pt-in **T**ext **E**ditor for **B**io-**O**ptically **O**rganized **K**nowledge, or NOTEBOOK for short. This revolutionary new storage device – the Dodo Blank Book - has no wires, no chips, no motherboards (or bored mothers), no crashes, no boots, no freezes. Sheets of wood pulp are bound and ordered sequentially. Each sheet is capable of storing thousands of bytes of information. The Dodo Blank Book works in all weathers and terrain from desert to tundra, temperate to arctic and is impervious to viruses, worms, magnetic fields and idiot operators. Could Michaelangelo have gone into ceiling design without one? Would Lord Dodo have remembered to pay the plumber to fix the Cistern in his Chapel? Did Einstein need a laptop for his Grand Unified Theory of Relatives? Where does your mother store her shopping list? Whether you're a budding Goya or Graffiti veteran, whether your calling is Grub Street or a Dusty Garret, whether your Grand Oeuvre is a Penny Dreadful or a Dollar Earner, or your Concerto for One Band Napping a hit or a miss, the Dodo Blank Book will always be at hand to save your ruminations and musings from oblivion. *Size: 6" x 8½" 160 pages*

Dodon't-Forget... the jogging range

NEW - The Dodo Door Pad - Out of sorts, but not out of doors? Then get a handle on your affairs and hang out your troubles and wares, lists and memos for all to see. It's time to let Lord Dodo show you the door with this hang-it-out-to-dodo memory jogger. *Size: 9" x 3¾" 75 sheets*

NEW - Dodo Sticky Notes

Do Do Remember: Dodon't-Forget-me-Notes. 4 sticky notepads of 50 pages each with a FREE postcard.

DODON'T FORGET this old favourite...

Memo Board - Magnetic, wipe-clean-memo-doodle-board with clip-on felt-tip pen.
5¾" x 6¾"

Download the lowdown at www.dodopad.com

Dodetachable order form

Name (please PRINT)

Address

Postcode / Zip   Tel No *(in case of query)*   Day/Eve

E-mail

Dodon't Forget Range & Dodorganisers		No. required	£ Total
DBB	NEW! Dodo Blank Book @ £8.95		
SNP	NEW! Dodo Sticky Notes (4 pads) @ £7.50		
DHP	NEW! Dodo Door Pad @ £5.50		
MMB	Wipe-clean Memo Board @ £4.50		
DTL	Dodo Travel Log @ £16.50		
DGB	Dodo Book of Garden Cuttings @ £17.95		
DBC	Dodo Book for Cooks @ £17.95		
ADB	Maxi Dodo Address Book @ £12.95 NEW DURABLE COVER!		
ADBM	Mini Dodo Address Book @ £8.50 NEW DURABLE COVER!		
DDP06	2006 Dodo Pad @ £11.95		
DWP06	2006 Dodo Wall Pad @ £11.95		
DDPM06	2006 Mini Dodo Pad @ £7.25		

Dodo Proverbial Mugs in Bone China @ £7.75			No. required	£ Total
DMS	Mug – Spanish	*How beautiful it is to do…*		
DMF	Mug – French	*It's always the impossible…*		
DMA	Mug – African	*Cross the river before you…*		
DMC	Mug – Chinese	*The birds of sadness…*		
DMU	Mug – American	*Some days you're the…*		
DMJ	Mug – Japanese	*Daylight will peep through…*		
DMB	Mug – Barbadian	*The new broom sweeps…*		
DMI	Mug – Irish	*Take the drink for the…*		
DMY	Mug – Yiddish	*One chops the wood…*		
DMM	Mug – Madagascan	*Don't think of the shortness…*		
DMG	Mug – Chinese	*All gardeners know better…*		
DML	Mug – Old Lore	*Pray to God but keep rowing…*		

Greetings Cards – order in multiples of 3 – mix & match at your whim!

☐ A – Spanish	☐ B – French	☐ C – African	☐ D – Chinese	3 @ £4.95
☐ E – American	☐ F – Japanese	☐ G – Barbadian	☐ H – Irish	6 @ £9.90
☐ J – Yiddish	☐ K – Madagascan	☐ L – Chinese	☐ M – Old Lore	9 @ £14.85
				12 @ £18.00

Please see below for Overseas Postage Supplements*

All prices shown above are <u>inclusive</u> of UK delivery. *Overseas postage supplements:
Please add £1.75 per copy/item for non-UK European mail and world-wide surface mail.
Add £2.75 per copy/item for world-wide airmail. NB: Greetings Cards do not attract
postage supplements. Bulk order prices on application.

Grand Total £

I enclose a crossed cheque/postal order payable to *The Dodo Pad Ltd*
OR Please debit my Visa/Mastercard/American Express/Switch account no:

(Switch only)

Start Date   Issue No.

Expiry date

USA and overseas orders: If you are paying with a non-UK credit card, your account will be
debited with the UK sterling equivalent at the time of order fulfilment.

Signature   Date

You can order from Lord Dodo in any of following ways:
Visit our web site: www.dodopad.com and order securely online
Order by e-mail: mailorder@dodopad.com

For dodoffice use only   05R

Mail Order telephone hotline: 0870 900 8004 (BT national call rates apply)
Order by post: The Dodo Pad, PO Box 34330, London, NW6 2RJ
Order by Fax: +44 (0) 870 750 3051 (BT national call rates apply)
We aim to dispatch within 7 days of receipt of your order but please allow up to 21 days for delivery. Subject to availability.

DIARY PRODUCE WITH A TOUCH OF SPICE

ZESTY:
THE DODOPAD

Britain's only free-range diary. The Dodorganizing Original is still the Best and full of Zest.

You asked for it! The Dodo Pad now comes with the revolutionary 'dodoPod' – a new stuff and store pouch for clippings, cuttings, memos and ephemera.

ZIPPY:
THE MINI DODOPAD

small and just as original, it zips into pockets and bags.

ZINGY:
THE WALLPAD

Calls from the Wall to all the family.

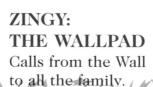

Handy new pouch to stuff and store essential bits of paper, bills etc. →

WHEREABOUTS WARE

MAXI: The Dodo Address Book
7¾" x 9¾"
MINI:
The Mini Dodo Address Book
4¼" x 5"

You can order from Lord Dodo in any of following ways:
Visit our web site: www.dodopad.com and order securely online
Order by e-mail: mailorder@dodopad.com
Mail Order telephone hotline: +44 (0)870 900 8004 (BT national call rates apply)
Order by post: The Dodo Pad, PO Box 34330, London, NW6 2RJ
Order by Fax: +44 (0) 870 750 3051 (BT national call rates apply)

FOR INTERNATIONAL, NATIONWIDE AND LOCAL STOCKISTS CALL THE HOTLINE

Download the lowdown at www.dodopad.com

Sharp Cards & Proverbial Mugs

GREETINGS CARDS – Twelve designs featuring unusual proverbs gathered from around the globe. Illustrated with Lord Dodo's inimitable wit and wisdom, the cards are suitable for many occasions. Blank inside for your own message. Available in multiples of 3 – mix and match at your whim! Size: 5" x 7"

Choose any 3 @ £4.95 or buy 12 of your choice @ £18.00 and save 10%

MUGS – Bone china mugs from Lord Dodo in blue, yellow and white.
(see order form for prices)

A: 'How beautiful it is to do nothing and then rest afterwards' *(Old Spanish Proverb)*

E: 'Some days you're the statue and some days you're the pigeon' *(Old American Proverb)*

J: 'One chops the wood – the other does the grunting' *(Old Yiddish Proverb)*

B: 'It is always the impossible that happens' *(Old French Proverb)*

F: 'Daylight will peep through a very small hole' *(Old Japanese Proverb)*

K: 'Don't think of the shortness of the day but of the length of the year' *(Old Madagascan Proverb)*

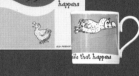

C: 'Cross the river before you abuse the crocodile' *(Old African Proverb)*

G: 'The new broom sweeps clean but the old broom knows the corners' *(Old Barbadian Proverb)*

L: 'All gardeners know better than other gardeners' *(another Old Chinese Proverb)*

D: 'The birds of sadness may fly overhead but don't let them nest in your hair' *(Old Chinese Proverb)*

H: 'Take the drink for the thirst that is yet to come' *(Old Irish Proverb)*

M: 'Pray to God but keep rowing to the shore' *(Old Lore)*

Download the lowdown at www.dodopad.com

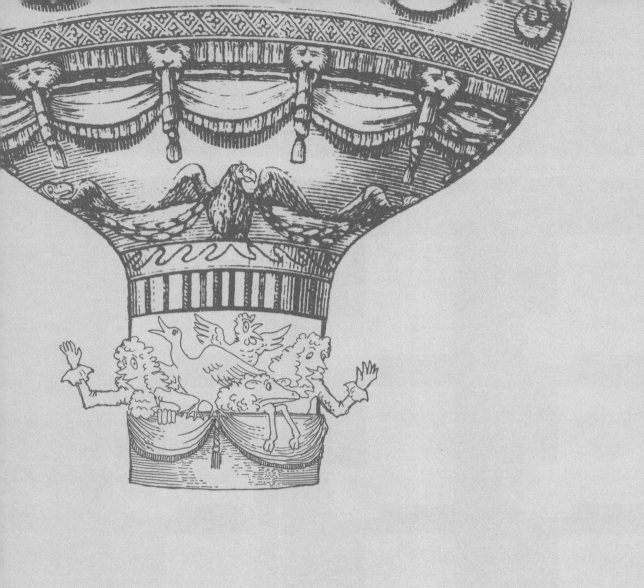

September

2005

19
Monday

1783 First manned hot air balloon ascent by the Montgolfier brothers

20
Tuesday

21
Wednesday

Autumn Equinox

22
Thursday

23
Friday

24
Saturday

25
Sunday

Louis XVI and Marie Antoinette watched the ascent. Also on
board were a cock, a goose and a sheep. All landed safely,
though the cock was kicked by the sheep.

The Dodo-Pad Sales Staff stripped for action.

* Lord Dodo has carefully checked his dodog-eared Dictionary of Ancient Greek, and can confirm that this reads 'Are you ready, girls? Let's get going!'

·SEPTEMBER·
·OCTOBER·
·2005·

26 Monday

27 Tuesday

28 Wednesday

29 Thursday

30 Friday

OCT 1 OBER Saturday

2 Sunday

1687 The Parthenon severely damaged by mortar bomb fired by Venetian army

Fair Greece! Sad relic of departed worth!
Immortal, though no more; though fallen, great!
Lord Byron

'ear, 'ear ...

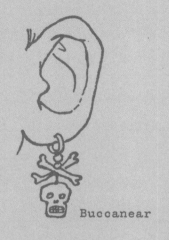

Buccanear

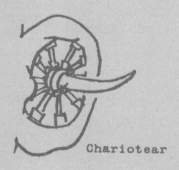

Chariotear

Gondolear

What do the following words have in common?

BRUNCH   CHORTLE   FLIMSY   SQUASH

Answers below October 30th

October
2005

3
Monday

●

4
Tuesday

Rosh Hashanah

Ramadan begins

5
Wednesday

6
Thursday

Feastday of St Bruno, who founded the Carthusian Order in 1084 at the Grande Chartreuse near Grenoble

7
Friday

8
Saturday

9
Sunday

What Heau!

My goodness, said Greuze,
Things are going from bad to weuze.
Rubbish, retorted Watteau;
I think you must be blatteau.

Beachcomber
(J.B. Morton)

October
2005

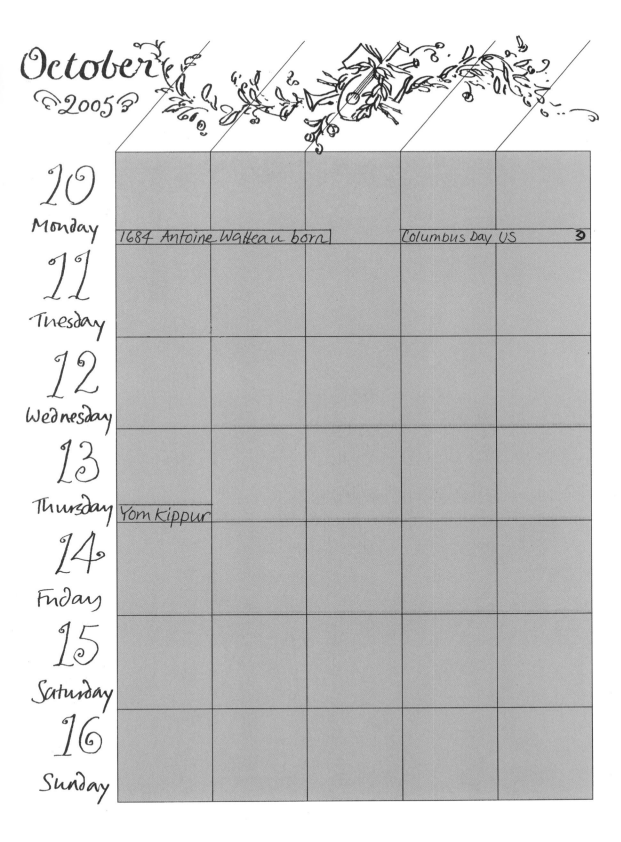

10 Monday — 1684 Antoine Watteau born | Columbus Day US ☽

11 Tuesday

12 Wednesday

13 Thursday — Yom Kippur

14 Friday

15 Saturday

16 Sunday

ENGLAND EXPECTS THAT EVERY MAN WILL DO HIS DUTY

October 2005

17 Monday

18 Tuesday

19 Wednesday

20 Thursday

21 Friday

1805 Battle of Trafalgar and death of Nelson

22 Saturday

23 Sunday

"Victory! Or Westminster Abbey!"

Nelson

STAN'S HOUR

Does killing time damage eternity?

OCTOBER 2005

24 Monday

Labour Day N.Z.

25 Tuesday

26 Wednesday

27 Thursday

28 Friday

29 Saturday

30 Sunday

British Summer Time ends

Answer: all these words were inventions
by Lewis Carroll

400th Anniversary of the Gunpowder Plot

A plot – or a Editorial meeting for the 1606 Dodo Pad?

October/
November
2005

31
Monday

Holiday Republic of Ireland

1
Tuesday

Diwali   All Saints Day

2
Wednesday

3
Thursday

4
Friday

5
Saturday

Guy Fawkes Night

6
Sunday

Lord Dodo of Doodle has generously agreed to leave this page bereft of his pearls of wisdom so that Dodopaddlers everywhere may start their Christmas lists!

But he would like to make one suggestion....

THE IDEAL PRESENT

NOVEMBER 2005

DANGER! CHRISTMAS AHEAD

7 Monday

8 Tuesday

9 Wednesday

10 Thursday

1871 Dr Livingstone found by Stanley

11 Friday

Veterans' Day US

12 Saturday

13 Sunday

Remembrance Sunday

One line alone has no meaning;
a second one is needed to give it expression.
Delacroix

Nov
2005

14 Monday

15 Tuesday

16 Wednesday

1960 Clark Gable died

O

17 Thursday

18 Friday

19 Saturday

20 Sunday

POPC

Blackbeard met his end in hand-to-hand combat
with Lt.Robert Maynard of HMS Pearl, who had
been commissioned to capture the notorious
pirate dead or alive.
Blackbeard's head was then suspended from the
Pearl's bowsprit.

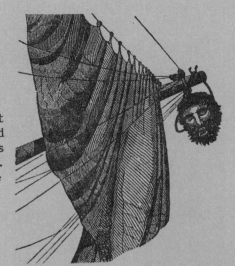

Blackbeard fumes when he discovers
that his second-in-command has
forgotten to order next year's Dodo Pad.
Trouble ahead!

NOVEMBER 2005

21 Monday

22 Tuesday

1718 Death of Blackbeard the Pirate

23 Wednesday

24 Thursday

Thanksgiving U.S.

25 Friday

26 Saturday

27 Sunday

Some dodistracting road signs have been spotted in the environs of Dodo Towers.....

DANGER
Pedestrians crossing ahead

"Would you like an omelette?", she asked eggregiously.

"Only if you've got the thyme", Tom replied asherbically.

"I'll make it when I've finished the housework", she choretled.

November/ December 2005

28 Monday

29 Tuesday

30 Wednesday

1 Thursday — 1135 King Henry I dies from a surfeit of lampreys

2 Friday

3 Saturday

4 Sunday

The Dearly Dodeparted Memorial Page

for those who have gone on ahead

HERE LIES in a horizontal Position the Outside Case of Geo. Roughleigh, Watchmaker whse abilities in that Line were an Honour to his Profession; Integrity was the Mainspring and Prudence the Regulator of all his Actions of his Life.... His Hand never Stopped till he had relieved Distress.. He departed this Life Nov 14, 1802, aged 57, Wound Up in Hopes of Being taken in Hand by his Maker and of being thoroughly Cleaned and Repaired and Set A-going in the —— World to Come ——

Lydford Church, Devon

A Dodopadling mother overheard her sons burying their dodeceased pet mouse...

"In the name of the father, and the son, and into the hole he goes"

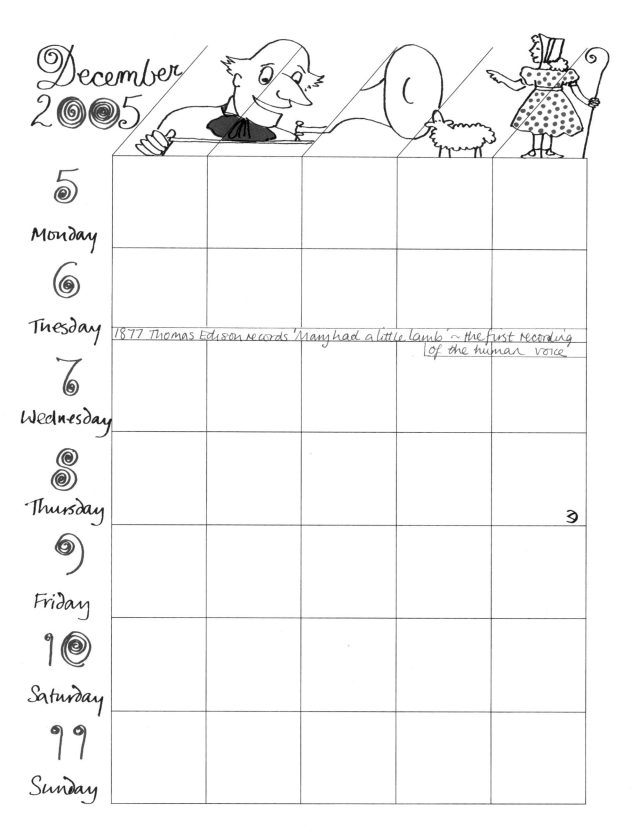

December
2005

5
Monday

6
Tuesday

1877 Thomas Edison records 'Mary had a little lamb' ~ the first recording of the human voice

7
Wednesday

8
Thursday

9
Friday

10
Saturday

11
Sunday

Epitaph for a waiter:- God finally caught his eye.

Madness finally overtakes those foolish enough
not to order their Dodo Pads in good time. . .

DECEMBER
2005

12
Monday

1863 Edvard Munch, Norwegian painter, born

13
Tuesday

14
Wednesday

15
Thursday

O

16
Friday

17
Saturday

18
Sunday

An awkward moment at the FUDPE* Christmas toga party.
Lord Dodo asks Miss Peabody to dodance, and she
discovers that her toga, imperfectly fastened, has
become irrevocably entangled with her chair.

* Federated Union of Dodo Pad Employees

2005

DECEMBER

19 Monday

20 Tuesday

21 Wednesday — Winter Solstice

22 Thursday

23 Friday

24 Saturday

25 Sunday — Christmas Day | Hanukkah

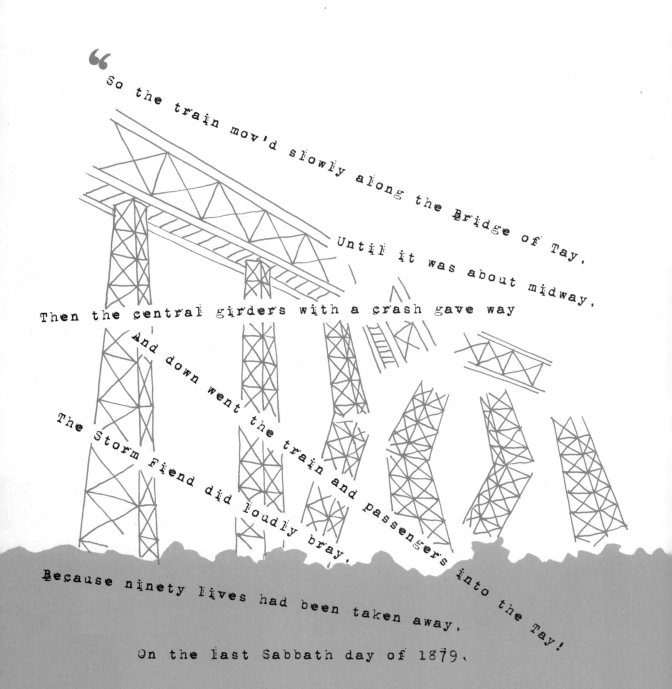

"So the train mov'd slowly along the Bridge of Tay,
Until it was about midway,
Then the central girders with a crash gave way
And down went the train and passengers into the Tay!
The Storm Fiend did loudly bray,
Because ninety lives had been taken away,
On the last Sabbath day of 1879,

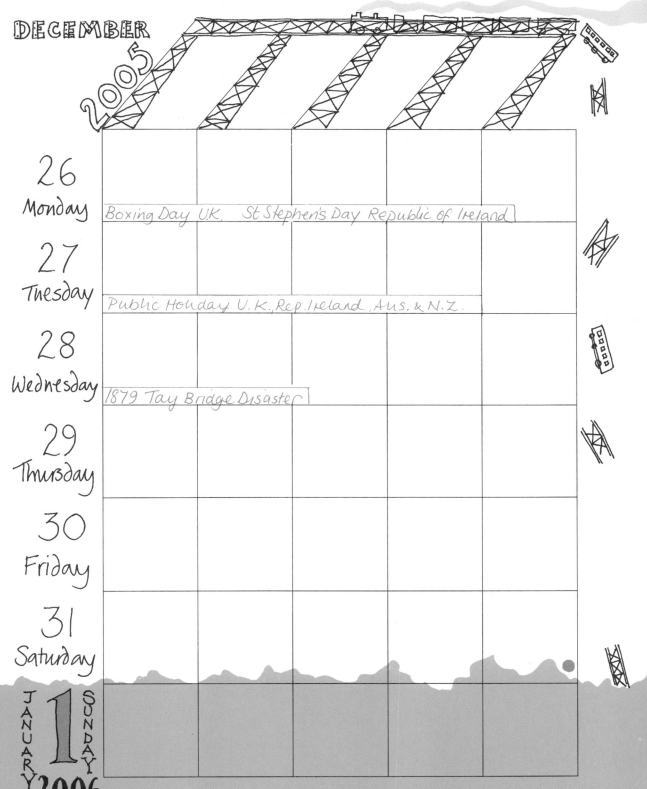

DECEMBER 2005

26 Monday	Boxing Day U.K. St Stephen's Day Republic of Ireland
27 Tuesday	Public Holiday U.K., Rep. Ireland, Aus. & N.Z.
28 Wednesday	1879 Tay Bridge Disaster
29 Thursday	
30 Friday	
31 Saturday	
JANUARY 1 SUNDAY 2006	

Which will be remember'd for a very long time.

William McGonagall

FORWARD

PLANNER ▶

January **2006**

february

march

april

16th April Easter Sunday

may

JUNE

NEW! FORWARD PLANNER 2006

JANUARY 2006

1 Su	NEW YEAR'S DAY	17 T	
2 M	PUBLIC HOLIDAY, NZ	18 W	
3 T		19 Th	
4 W		20 F	
5 Th		21 S	
6 F		22 Su	
7 S		23 M	
8 Su		24 T	
9 M		25 W	
10 T		26 Th	AUSTRALIA DAY
11 W		27 F	
12 Th		28 S	
13 F		29 Su	
14 S		30 M	
15 Su		31 T	
16 M	MARTIN LUTHER KING DAY (U.S.)		

FEBRUARY 2006

1 W		17 F	
2 Th		18 S	
3 F		19 Su	
4 S		20 M	PRESIDENT'S DAY (U.S.)
5 Su		21 T	
6 M	WAITANGI DAY, NZ	22 W	
7 T		23 Th	
8 W		24 F	
9 Th		25 S	
10 F		26 Su	
11 S		27 M	
12 Su		28 T	
13 M			
14 T			
15 W			
16 Th			

Public Holidays et al.
This information is correct at time of going to press. The publishers accept no responsibility for any errors.

MARCH 2006

1 W		17 F	ST. PATRICK'S DAY
2 Th		18 S	
3 F		19 Su	
4 S		20 M	
5 Su		21 T	
6 M		22 W	
7 T		23 Th	
8 W		24 F	
9 Th		25 S	
10 F		26 Su	
11 S		27 M	
12 Su		28 T	
13 M	COMMONWEALTH DAY, AUS	29 W	
14 T		30 Th	
15 W		31 F	
16 Th			

APRIL 2006

1 S		17 M	EASTER MONDAY
2 Su		18 T	
3 M		19 W	
4 T		20 Th	
5 W		21 F	
6 Th		22 S	
7 F		23 Su	
8 S		24 M	
9 Su		25 T	ANZAC DAY
10 M		26 W	
11 T		27 Th	
12 W		28 F	
13 Th	PASSOVER	29 S	
14 F	GOOD FRIDAY	30 Su	
15 S			
16 Su	EASTER SUNDAY		

MAY 2006

1 M	MAY HOLIDAY, UK + REP. IRELAND	17 W	
2 T		18 Th	
3 W		19 F	
4 Th		20 S	
5 F		21 Su	
6 S		22 M	
7 Su		23 T	
8 M		24 W	
9 T		25 Th	
10 W		26 F	
11 Th		27 S	
12 F		28 Su	
13 S		29 M	MEMORIAL DAY (U.S.) BANK HOLIDAY, UK
14 Su		30 T	
15 M		31 W	
16 T			

JUNE 2006

1 Th		17 S	
2 F		18 Su	
3 S		19 M	
4 Su		20 T	
5 M	QUEEN'S BIRTHDAY, NZ HOLIDAY REP. IRELAND	21 W	
6 T		22 Th	
7 W		23 F	
8 Th		24 S	
9 F		25 Su	
10 S		26 M	LABOUR DAY, NZ
11 Su		27 T	
12 M		28 W	
13 T		29 Th	
14 W		30 F	
15 Th			
16 F			

NEW! FORWARD PLANNER 2006

JULY 2006

1 S		17 M	
2 Su		18 T	
3 M		19 W	
4 T	INDEPENDENCE DAY, USA	20 Th	
5 W		21 F	
6 Th		22 S	
7 F		23 Su	
8 S		24 M	
9 Su		25 T	
10 M		26 W	
11 T		27 Th	
12 W	HOLIDAY, N. IRELAND	28 F	
13 Th		29 S	
14 F		30 Su	
15 S		31 M	
16 Su			

AUGUST 2006

1 T		17 Th	
2 W		18 F	
3 Th		19 S	
4 F		20 Su	
5 S		21 M	
6 Su		22 T	
7 M	HOLIDAY, SCOTLAND + REP. IRELAND	23 W	
8 T		24 Th	
9 W		25 F	
10 Th		26 S	
11 F		27 Su	
12 S		28 M	BANK HOLIDAY, UK
13 Su		29 T	
14 M		30 W	
15 T		31 Th	
16 W			

SEPTEMBER 2006

1 F		17 Su	
2 S		18 M	
3 Su		19 T	
4 M	LABOR DAY, USA	20 W	
5 T		21 Th	
6 W		22 F	
7 Th		23 S	ROSH HASHANAH
8 F		24 Su	RAMADAN BEGINS
9 S		25 M	
10 Su		26 T	
11 M		27 W	
12 T		28 Th	
13 W		29 F	
14 Th		30 S	
15 F			
16 S			

OCTOBER 2006

1 Su		17 T	
2 M	YOM KIPPUR	18 W	
3 T		19 Th	
4 W		20 F	
5 Th		21 S	DIWALI
6 F		22 Su	
7 S		23 M	
8 Su		24 T	
9 M	COLUMBUS DAY (U.S.)	25 W	
10 T		26 Th	
11 W		27 F	
12 Th		28 S	
13 F		29 Su	
14 S		30 M	HOLIDAY, REP. IRELAND
15 Su		31 T	
16 M			

NOVEMBER 2006

1 W		17 F	
2 Th		18 S	
3 F		19 Su	
4 S		20 M	
5 Su		21 T	
6 M		22 W	
7 T		23 Th	THANKSGIVING, USA
8 W		24 F	
9 Th		25 S	
10 F		26 Su	
11 S	VETERANS' DAY (U.S.)	27 M	
12 Su		28 T	
13 M		29 W	
14 T		30 Th	
15 W			
16 Th			

DECEMBER 2006

1 F		17 Su	
2 S		18 M	
3 Su		19 T	
4 M		20 W	
5 T		21 Th	
6 W		22 F	
7 Th		23 S	
8 F		24 Su	
9 S		25 M	CHRISTMAS DAY
10 Su		26 T	BOXING DAY
11 M		27 W	
12 T		28 Th	
13 W		29 F	
14 Th		30 S	
15 F	HANUKKAH	31 Su	
16 S			

The
Appendix

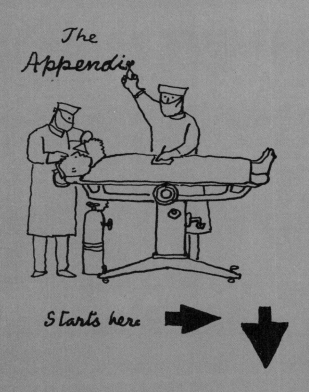

Starts here ➡ ⬇

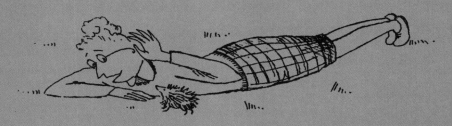

Miss Enid Bagthorpe, after further study, is _sure_ she hears the hedgehog reply.

Closeted in his eyrie on the 40th floor of Canadodo Tower, Lord Dodo's Sub-Editor-in-Chief scans the proofs for the merest suggestion of even the slightest infelicity or *mot unjuste* in the Fortieth Anniversary Issue of the venerable and indodispensable **2006 Dodo Pad**. Order your copy NOW to avoid despair, disappointment, or worse, dodeprivation.

Where am I? Who am I? How came I
here? What is this thing called the
world? What does this world mean? Who
is it that has lured me into this
thing and now leaves me there? Why
was I not consulted?

Kierkegaard

The Dodo-Pad doesn't pretend to answer any of those enormous questions,
only to take your mind off them.

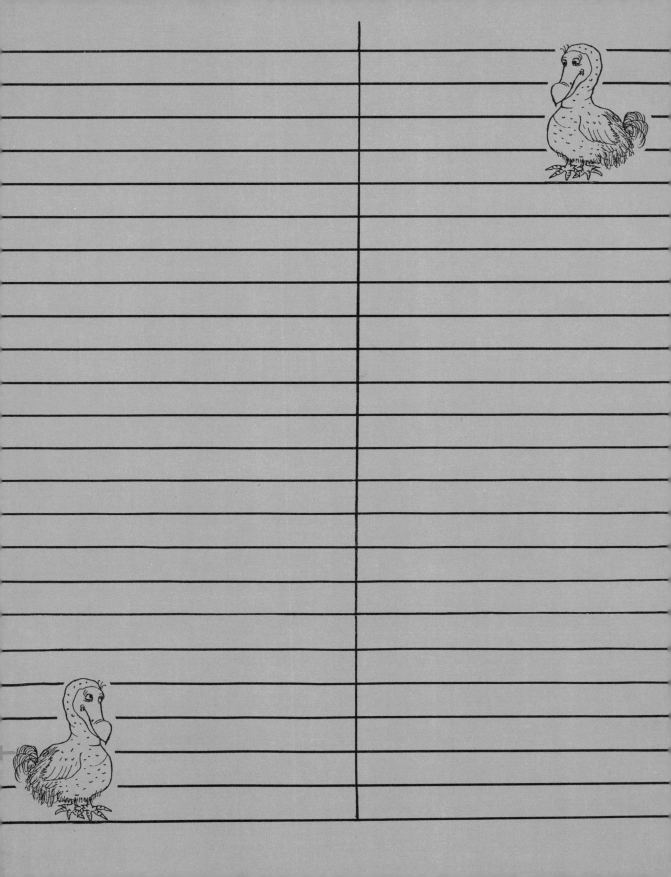